The Tree of Intimacy
And The Fruits of Love, Power, and Blessing

An Invitation to Revival

By: Brian Britton

Copyright © 2004 by Brian Britton

The Tree of Intimacy
by Brian Britton

Printed in the United States of America

ISBN 1-594676-78-X

All rights reserved solely by the author. The author guarantees all contents are original and do not infringe upon the legal rights of any other person or work. No part of this book may be reproduced in any form without the permission of the author. The views expressed in this book are not necessarily those of the publisher.

Unless otherwise indicated, Bible quotations are taken from the New American Standard Bible. Copyright © 1995 by World Publishing.

www.xulonpress.com

This book is dedicated to my wonderful wife, Valerie.
You are truly the greatest blessing and gift in my life.
Thank you for your amazing love and support.
It is such a joy to walk through this life with you.

Contents

- I. Foreword ix
- II. Introduction: There Must Be More! xi
- III. Part One: The Tree of Intimacy 17
- IV. Part Two: The Fruit of Love 31
- V. Part Three: The Fruit of Power 43
- VI. Part Four: The Fruit of Blessing 63
- VII. Invitation To Revival 73

Foreword

This book, *The Tree of Intimacy*, more than lives up to its title. It is a remarkable book by a very bright and promising young man, Brian Britton. I met Brian when he was a student in the School of Divinity at Regent University where I serve as Dean. I was initially impressed with his energy and vision. He is sincere, anointed, and has a burning vision for world evangelism. Unlike many aspiring evangelists who see little value in education and preparation for ministry, Brian set a goal early on, to learn as much as he could before he entered full-time ministry.

Even so, he found time to conduct mass crusades in Nigeria, Russia, and Brazil while he was still in seminary. His wife, Valerie, a native of Russia and also a seminary graduate, shares his vision and is a wonderful helpmeet to him. Together, they make a marvelous team.

The subtitle of the book, "the fruits of love, power, and blessing" define the contents of the work. It is partly autographical and gives insight into the experiences and vision that explains much about Brian and his life goals. It is written out of youthful vision, full of love, energy, and a depth of maturity beyond his years. It is, as he says, a powerful "invitation to revival."

Vinson Synan
Regent University
June 17, 2004

Introduction

There Must Be More!

During my first year of seminary, I spent a lot of time in prayer asking God to give to me more clarity regarding the calling upon my life. Honestly, most of what was being shown to me I did not fully understand at the time, but the one thing I did understand, was that I had to go somewhere and share the gospel of Jesus Christ. There was a message inside of me that just had to get out. I also believe the Lord said to me that "I will use you to tell my children I love them, and I will show them." During this same year, I had a vision where I saw myself touching a sick person and lifting up their face until I could look them in the eyes, then I just said "Jesus loves you" and something inside me knew they were healed and had been touched by God.

    The next year, while still in seminary, I had the opportunity to travel with a team from my church on a short-term missions trip to Russia. While there, I was given the opportunity to preach in a local church in St. Petersburg, and at a small service at a drug rehab center. During both meetings, the Lord blessed many people. At the rehab center, many gave their lives to Christ, and at the local church, a few people were healed during the time of ministry. Needless to say, I was very encouraged and was growing daily in my walk with the Lord and my understanding of how His Spirit worked through His people.

In a couple of months, I traveled to Nigeria to preach at a series of evangelistic crusades. Imagine my surprise when I stepped off the plane in Lagos and saw my friend Pastor John Iseghohi holding a huge poster with my face on it that read, "The blind see, the deaf hear, the lame walk, and the dead are raised!" To make matters a little more intense, as we drove around the city where the crusade was to be held, these posters, and my face, were all over the place. I mean on just about every building! Well, to make a long story short, I really spent a lot of time between the meetings on my knees crying out to God that when I preached, He would show up and touch His people. Praise the Lord that we did have many salvations and healings as the gospel was preached. And to His glory they invited me back the following year for another set of meetings. When we go in His name, and by His leading, He always shows up and confirms His Word.

As wonderful as all this was to me, a young man just beginning in doing the Lord's work, I knew that something was missing. During and after these times of ministry, I always sensed that God wanted to do more. I plainly saw when reading the scriptures that it was God's will to heal the sick and oppressed. I knew that to reach this generation we needed to proclaim a living Jesus in such a way that could not be denied by this world. I sensed that the Lord wanted to literally pour His goodness, love, and power upon His children, but for some reason, there seemed to be something hampering this move of God.

As God so often does, He used my wife Valerie to bring a revelation of His will into my life. You see, at the time I was beginning to travel to these nations and preach, I was studying the ministries of other men and women that God was using in a way in which I felt similarly called to minister. I spent hours reading books about God's power and anointing. The Lord used these books to teach me a great deal about what I was seeing and what to expect overseas and at home during times of ministry. More than anything else, I wanted to see this move of God that was happening overseas in places like Nigeria and Argentina come to America. After all,

The Tree of Intimacy

---

didn't God love all people and nations the same?

My wife Valerie and I met in seminary at Regent University in Virginia Beach, Virginia. She is from Moscow, Russia and for about seven years before she came to the United States to study and prepare for full-time ministry, she served as an interpreter for many ministries as they would come to Russia. Being in Moscow, a city of around 13 million, she was blessed to attend and assist with conferences and meetings by many well know international ministries. One of these conferences she attended was conducted by a man named Jack Frost. Jack and his wife Trisha have founded Shiloh Place Ministries and they travel the world ministering out of their revelation of the Father's Heart and Love.

Well, one day we get a package from Valerie's mother in Moscow, and inside are some tapes of this Father's Love conference in Moscow. At first, very ashamedly, I was not really interested in another teaching on "love." I was only interested in experiencing more of God's power and the fire of His Holy Spirit being manifest in my life. I was making a mistake that many Christians do by focusing on one aspect of the gospel and thinking that it was all I needed to know. But our gospel is a full and complete gospel, and as I was soon to be reminded, it cannot be full and complete without a true revelation of the Father's love.

Well, I reluctantly agreed to listen to the tapes on the way to work. I remember thinking how funny and ironic it was that I was listening to tapes from Russia of a minister from South Carolina! To my surprise, during the first tape I was captured by the power of the message, and during a time of prayer that soon followed, I was blessed with a deeper understanding of God's amazing love.

A few month's later, a man named James Jordan who has a wonderful ministry with his wife Denise in New Zealand, came to minister at a conference at our local church in Virginia. During the conference, which was truly great, I really didn't feel that I had received all that God wanted to reveal to me. So, that evening when we got home I laid out in the floor of our study and cried out to God for more of His love and for more of His presence in my life. For more intimacy with Him. I stayed there on the floor, for over and hour as God revealed to me more and more of His love for me and

The Tree of Intimacy

for all His children.

About a month later, I was ministering in the island nation of Malta in a small church. At the end of the service, a young woman came forward. As I was praying for her, I lifted her face up and asked her to look up at me. As she did, I realized that I really loved her. The Lord had given me a special glimpse of His love for her in that moment. As I laid hands on her for prayer I did so out of the same compassion that Jesus ministered in. I immediately was given discernment into her situation in life and when I told her that Jesus loved her, she looked into my eyes and saw the love of Jesus! She saw it was for real, and God touched her and set her free from a spirit of depression that had plagued her and her family for generations!

Three months later, I was in Brazil for a series of crusades and meetings in Parana, State. God moved greatly in every city we were in, but in the last city, on the last night, something special happened. After the message, I felt that God wanted to heal those that had pain in their bodies. When I gave the call to come forward for those who wanted to be healed, about 50 people came to the front of the stage of the gymnasium in the city of Laranjeiras do Sul.

The night before, there had been a powerful time of prophetic ministry and I had personally laid hands and prayed for about 200 people. So, this night, I began to pray for and lay hands on each of those who were in pain. Again, as in Malta, when I prayed for these people I looked into their eyes, I touched them, and I really loved them. I was filled with God's love for them. And again, when they looked into my eyes they saw it was real. That night all but two people were healed in that gym. For the first time in my life I actually felt things physically move inside of people when I prayed for them. I had felt the Lord touch people before in prayer, usually with a feeling of heat, but never like this and never such a large percentage of the group.

That night, in the hotel, I thanked God for allowing me to be a part of what He just did. He then began to show me some very important principles. These principles are what this book is really all about, and they hinge on this statement: Without a true revelation of God's love in your life, no matter what you have, you really have nothing. Earlier in my ministry, I had laid hands on the sick in

The Tree of Intimacy

the name of Jesus because I thought that was what God wanted me to do. I did it because the Bible tells us to, and I believe the Bible is the Word of God. I thought that I was supposed to tell them about God's love and then just let Him love them. I gave because I knew it was God's will for me to give, and when I gave I wanted to please my God, whom I loved more than anything on earth. But I believe that there is more that God is calling His church to do today. Yes, God wants us to bless others, and yes God wants us to give, and yes God wants to manifest His power in a way that has never been seen upon this earth. But He wants to use us to do it. And He can only use us fully, when we first have a revelation of His love for us, and when we genuinely have a love for this world that is dying, hurting and needs Him so desperately.

It is my desire to show you that you cannot separate the awesome, awe inspiring power of God, from the amazing, incredible love of the Father. From this love and from this power being manifested in and through us, will come an abundance of God's blessing in our lives. We are called to bless this world. I also want to show you that we can not have a true revelation of the Father's love unless we have extended times of intimacy dwelling in His presence. We have all heard the almost cliché expression "You can have as much of God in your life as you want." I want you to know that it is true and not to be taken for granted. God wants to manifest His power in a way that will shake the nations, but I am convinced it will never happen until we have His heart, and His eyes, and His compassion, as a result of a lifestyle of intimacy with Him.

In the following chapters I will explain how intimacy with God brings forth the fruits of love, power and blessing. It is my belief that this great love and power that we will see poured out upon the face of the earth will usher in the mighty end-time move of God we have all heard so much about. This revival will be a result of a generation that will be raised up to be extremely intimate with Him. It is my desire that this book will serve as an invitation to this revival. That through it God might say "Come to Me, come to Me my glorious bride, come to Me and enjoy the refreshing I have for you and finally walk in all the power and authority that I have intended for you."

So now let us look to God's Word and other examples of how we can flow in the fullness of the divine destiny that God has for His church. Let's examine together the topics of intimacy, love, power, and blessing, in hopes that we can soon allow the kingdom of God to fully take over our lives and ministries.

Part One

The Tree of Intimacy

Intimacy with Him Is a Necessity

I believe that it is the heart of God for the church today that we realize that intimacy with the Father is an absolute necessity for every aspect of our lives and ministry. We cannot fulfill the plans He has for His glorious end-times Bride unless we are regularly in His presence. The Bible instructs us to pursue Him, and promises us that if we do, we shall indeed find Him. My favorite verse in all of scripture deals with this promise. Matthew 5:6 reads, *"Blessed are those who hunger and thirst for righteousness, for they shall be satisfied (filled)."* He tells us again, *"seek and you shall find, knock and the door shall be opened."*[1]

What wonderful promises from the lips of Jesus Christ Himself! He is not hiding from us, and as a matter of fact, He longs to be close to us. He has promised that He will never leave us or forsake us. Well, most of us know these promises backwards and forwards. The question I challenge you to answer today is, "Are you regularly spending time in His presence?" Are you consumed with a desire to find Him as David was when he penned Psalm 63:1, *"O God, You are my God; I shall seek You earnestly; my soul thirsts for You, my flesh yearns for you...?"*

Do we understand that God created us for fellowship with Himself? This was His intention from the beginning of time. In the garden He walked with Adam in the cool of the day, and He longs to walk with you and I in the same way. Many of us do understand these scriptures mentally, but do we really believe them in our heart? For the church to fulfill its end time destiny we must purpose to seek Him as never before. There must arise a cry of desperation from within the Body of Christ that longs to know Him on a more extreme and intimate level. I believe that the Lord will use this book and others like it to sound a trumpet for His glorious Bride to seek Him, no longer just for what He can do for us, but for who He is. There is a difference. Not just crying out for His blessing, but crying out wantingly for Him and His presence. Crying out that we might see His glory in our generation.

I believe that He has called and set apart this generation for a new level of intimacy. God is looking to and fro across the earth for a people that are hungry for His glory. He is pouring out a revelation upon the church today that we continually have total access to the throne room of God almighty. We are at all times in His midst. I have heard it said that in Heaven everyone will be seeking to get before the throne. That throne is the "place to be" in heaven, and it is a place we have access to today if we would only believe!

We are truly on the verge of a movement that will shake the nations for God's glory. Are we desperate in our churches that such a movement might begin? I believe that the Holy Spirit has led me to write this book not just to fill a place on your bookshelf, but that the flames that He has already put in your heart will be fanned, and that this movement will begin with you. I am writing this that you might hear what I believe is the heart of God for our generation and be forever changed. That by reading you would be moved to action.

He Is Always Speaking To Us

Intimacy with God comes from a deep desire to be with him on a minute by minute basis. Again, most of us understand that we can

The Tree of Intimacy

converse with God continually, but are we truly doing this as frequently and with the passion that we should? On the other side of the coin, some of you right now may be thinking, I don't even know for sure that I can hear God's voice at all. I want to share with you a little experiment that will help you to realize that you can and do hear the voice of God if you are baptized in the Holy Spirit.

In Brazil this year, I was approached by a young minister of the gospel who shared with me his uncertainty about hearing the voice of God. I shared only what I had learned during my own daily journey with the Lord. I asked Him, "When you are in prayer and you ask the Lord to speak to you, what do you hear immediately?" Then I said, "Don't answer me, because I know what He says to you. I know what He says to you because He says the same thing to me and to everyone else who has ever asked that question of Him. The answer you always hear in your head is, "I am always speaking to you." He then said "That's right! That's what I hear."

The Lord is always speaking to us! His desire is that we be in constant communication with Him. The Word of God instructs us to "pray without ceasing."[2] Well, we need to know that prayer is a dialogue not a monologue. Prayer is more than us just bringing our needs and problems before God. Prayer also involves, waiting on Him and listening for His words of love and direction.

Once, in a time of prayer, the Lord gave me a picture in my mind of what our prayer life with Him is often like. I saw myself standing by a small waterfall. My right ear was very close to the water. Through the sound of the falling water I heard a muffled sound that was almost indistinguishable. Then something within me told me to lean in and put my head through the water. When I did, I was able to clearly hear a voice speaking to me, and when I turned my head to look in the direction from where the voice was coming, it was the Lord I saw speaking. This was a perfect picture of my own prayer life at the time. I was hearing only a tiny, muffled, filtered, amount of what the Lord was speaking to me. He desired for me to "lean in" or "press in" to get to where He was waiting and speaking to me. When I did this, I quickly moved into a season of clarity in respect to understanding God's direction for my life.

Children of God's Promises

I have always loved to read the stories in the Old Testament of God's promises. I must admit that many times, I would read the accounts of the lives of men like David and Abraham with a little bit of jealousy. God made such promises to these men! He used them so mightily. They walked so closely to Him. Let's take Abraham for instance. God said to Abraham in Genesis 12:1-3,

> *"Go forth from your country, and from your relatives, and from your fathers house, to the land which I will show you; and I will make you a great nation, and I will bless you, and make your name great; and so you shall be a blessing; and I will bless those who bless you, and the one who curses you I will curse. And in you all the families of the earth will be blessed."*

How's that for a word from the Lord! Imagine how Abraham must have felt after receiving such a word from God. Or how about David, when God told Him He would establish his kingdom forever? These men had covenant relationship with God. They had heard the voice of the Lord and they walked boldly into the future standing on His promise.

God is speaking to His church today. As a result of the death and resurrection of Jesus Christ, we are heirs of a much greater promise than either David or Abraham ever imagined. We are heirs to a promise that says He will be with us always, He will indwell us, He will walk side by side with us always and forever. The New Testament promise is a promise of an intimacy with the God of Abraham, Isaac, and Jacob that they would have given anything to walk in. This is the promise of all promises, that we might know Him, walk with Him, and be transformed into His very image.

Time invested in any relationship always leads to a better knowledge and understanding of the person you spend time with. In the same way, time spent with God results in an exponential knowledge of the things of His kingdom. You are a part of the generation that God has chosen to reveal His promises to in a fresh light that has never before been seen. We are the children of God's promise. The promise of extreme intimacy with Him.

Embracing The Silence

When you go to your secret, quiet place to meet with God, when you go to your prayer closet, do you find it an easy thing to do? Is it easy for you to sit in silence and solitude for any length of time? For most westerners, the answer to these questions is probably an emphatic "no!." We are scared to death of silence! One eastern observer remarked on his first visit to United States that "Americans seemed to have a need to surround themselves with noise all the time."[3] Not only that, but the average American professional who spends five minutes "doing nothing," feels guilty.

Stephen Foster devoted an entire chapter in his book, *Celebration of Discipline,* to solitude and silence. In it he says that silence is a discipline. Just as prayer and fasting and worship are disciplines to be cultivated in our lives, so also are silence and solitude. He also touches on the idea that when we are silent, we relinquish control of the situation we are in.[4] So, I now ask you this, if we are alone and praying, and we are silent, who do we relinquish control to? To God! He could and would take control if we would only let Him. Inside of us there may be a deeply hidden fear of letting God have total control. Of what will happen if we give it all to Him.

It may also be true that we just have a hard time not talking. For some of us it is a struggle to be quiet, even before the Lord. I know that when I pray I have a tendency to ramble. Sometimes I just have so much I want to bring to God in prayer. Things seem so dire, and I just need to tell Him this or that. Meanwhile, like the Father He is, He says to me "I know, I know, I will handle it, just lay it all down and trust me." And we sometimes refuse to drop it. We say, "But God, You don't understand how bad this is or how important this is!" Again He says, "Just give it to me. It's ok." And this goes on and on. Let me say this, His will for us is that we would bring it to Him and then just lay it down. There is a rest in His presence. He has a grace for you to be quiet and still before Him! As the Word of God says to us "Be still and know that I am God."[5] Pray with me today that as a church, we will cultivate a lifestyle of being able to be quiet before God. There is so much He is saying that He is waiting for us to hear.

Understanding God's Heart

Mike Bickle has recently written an excellent book entitled, *After God's Own Heart*, in which he writes extensively on the fascinating life of David. I highly recommend this book for anyone desiring a more intimate experience with God. He really has gleaned some amazing insights from God's Word, specifically regarding David and intimacy with the Father. One idea in this book that instantly captured my mind and heart, was how David's life was characterized by a great desire to understand God's heart and emotions. He writes "...he (David) became a student of God's emotions. He wanted to know what wonders, pleasures, and fearsome things filled God's heart." He also writes that David became a "scholar of God's affections."[6]

I don't know about you, but I pray that we too would desire to earnestly study the heart of God, and spend our waking moments pondering the depths of His affections. That we would know what moves Him, and what He loves. That we would understand Him in a way that no generation in the history of the church has ever dreamed possible! I believe that this is the generation that God is calling to just such a level of extreme intimacy. My heart burns with a passion to see into the very heart of God. How blessed is this generation that He has chosen for such an honor and time as this! His Spirit is a Spirit of truth, a Spirit that desires us to know the truth, and what could possibly be more true than the heart of God? Let the church cry out today that God would give us a burning desire to see into the secret places of His heart.

Shepherds Who know Their Master

One major problem in the church today, particularly in the west, is that we have men and women being sent out into full-time ministry that don't really know Jesus on an intimate level. This is especially true with those graduating from our seminaries. I know because it was not too long ago when I was a student myself.

Our western culture places a great deal of value on education, and rightly so. I am a firm believer that our leaders in the church need to have a rock solid theological foundation before being sent out to lead and guide their flocks, or to train other children of God in the classroom. I have seen too many well intentioned ministers mistakenly teach unbiblical doctrines to think otherwise. That said, a good seminary or Bible school education means nothing without a daily intimate walk with the Lord. There is absolutely no substitute for knowing Him intimately.

The difficult part, is that this lifestyle of intimacy with the Lord must be cultivated and pursued individually and outside of the classroom. During my time of seminary studies, I saw so many of my friends and colleagues struggle as a result of doing everything for God, but not really knowing Him. Without Him, all is in vain. We can have the best intentions and motivations, and even be truly called, but if we do not actively and passionately seek Him, we will be doing it for the most part in the power of the flesh rather than empowered by His Holy Spirit.

Intimacy Provides Nourishment

A lifestyle of intimacy with God provides much needed nourishment to our body and our spirit. When most of us think about nourishment, we think of food of some sort. Food gives us nourishment or fuel to go forward and live our lives. The better we are nourished, the more activities we are able to accomplish. Proper nourishment also brings about efficiency in the things that we do. The right fuel enables us to increase our output.

When we spend time with God, He increases our strength. As a meal would fill our bodies with calories, a time of intimacy with the Father empowers us to fulfill not only our daily activities, but also the purposes of God in our life.

Another aspect of this nourishment is direction. When we meet with Him and seek His direction for our lives, He is faithful to reveal His plans to us. A great example of this is found in the life of Jesus

Himself. In Luke 6:12 we read that before He picked the 12 disciples, "Jesus went out to the mountainside to pray, and spent the night praying to God." From this we can see that when Jesus had an important decision to make, He always sought the direction of His Father. How much more should we! In times of prayer and soaking in His presence, allow Him to nourish you, and watch as your daily energy level and efficiency begins to climb. Why rely just on sleep and physical food, when you have access to such a greater source of power?[7]

It's For Everyone!

God tells us to "Seek first His kingdom and His righteousness, and all these things will be added to you."[8] When we seek Him, we always find Him in all of His goodness. He is always there and has plenty to say to this generation. This radical intimacy with our Father is for everyone. In times past, many in the church have thought that such an intimacy with God was attainable only by those called to full-time vocational ministry or maybe "saints" of generations past.

Quite the contrary, it seems that across the world today there is a fresh revelation of God's desire for intimacy with all of His children. Prayer movements are springing up all over the world. In places like Kansas City's International House of Prayer we see men and women being called to 24 hour a day, round the clock prayer. From Korea, to China, to Africa, to the United States, God is birthing a desire in His church for a new level of intimacy with the Father. New songs are being penned by men and women the world over with lyrics crying out for intimacy with God. There seems to be an outpouring of anointing for songwriting upon the church that is unrivaled in it's history. And these new songs are not sung to a distant, far away God, but rather they are love songs to a very attainable and available Father.

I want to encourage you that it *is* possible to live a life continually in God's presence. When Jesus comes into our lives, He stays. The Holy Spirit takes up permanent residence inside us. Now, if He is indwelling our very bodies, are we allowing Him into every situation as we should? Do we talk to Him and acknowledge Him regularly? I heard the wonderful teacher and minister, John Bevere share once during a message an illustration that went something like this. Imagine you are driving in you car with a friend or family member. Would you totally ignore them for twenty minutes on the way to work? Most of you wouldn't even consider being so rude. You would at least acknowledge them and converse a little. Well, don't you know that the Lord of Heaven and Earth is right there with you on the way to work that ten or twenty minutes every morning? Do we really believe this? How often do we forget Him? How often are we too immersed in our own stuff to even acknowledge His presence with us in times like this throughout our cluttered lives. I want to assure you He is there, and He wants so very much to share your day with you.

God is looking all over the world for a people that will commit to being completely His. He wants you to just open your life to Him completely and continually, and to routinely lose yourself in His love. He wants you to reject any thoughts that distract you from Him. It is a necessity to be aware of His constant presence with us. We need to know that the thought that we must turn away from our conversation with the Father in order to deal with the details of our everyday lives is a lie from our enemy.[9] You can and should allow God into every situation in your life.

The secret to a successful Christian life is that you would accept His love and rejoice in Him. If you can do that, He will surely lead you into everything else He has ordained for your life. If you seek Him, you will not miss out on a single portion of your destiny that He created you for. Imagine, He loves you more than you do, and if you are listening to Him, He won't let you miss those moments that He has ordained for you to move in. When you are connected to Him, there is no need to worry. When the door of opportunity opens, you will be in the right place.

Intimacy with God means a complete surrender to Him of our lives, dreams, families, and ministries. When we lay them all before Him and quit our striving to fix everything ourselves, we will know the peace talked about in Scripture that "surpasses all understanding." This is not an easy thing to do for a lot of us. Pride usually keeps us from walking in this peace as soon as most of us would like.

Men especially have something ingrained in us that says we

must do everything ourselves. If there is a problem, we must fix it or find the way out. I feel that it is important to share that often when we find ourselves in a problem, the last thing we do is look to God. Why is this so hard even for some very mature Christians?

Desperate For Him

Not so long ago, my mother in-law Galina was visiting us from Moscow. During her stay, we asked her to lead our small group and she shared this wonderful picture the Lord showed her regarding this very problem. She said that she saw herself in a dark cave and that there was a labyrinth inside. No matter what she tried, she kept running into dead ends. It was just too dark and she knew she would never find the way out. There seemed to be no hope. Then suddenly she looked up and saw a great torch. The torch was putting off a light that lit up the whole cave. The light revealed that on the floor of the labyrinth there were actually arrows pointing to the way out!

Afterwards the Lord revealed to her the meaning of this picture or vision. When we are in a dark place, or a place of crisis, we waste precious time wandering around trying to find the way out ourselves. When we do this it seems we will never find the way out and get to where we know that God wants us to be. But when we look up to God, when we seek Him, we immediately see that He has already provided the way out. You see, God has a place He wants you to get to! He has a plan for you to fulfill, and unless we learn to come to Him, to seek "the light" first, we will spend Lord knows how long wandering around in the dark. A life lived in intimacy with Him is a light lived by the light of His torch. A life where we can more easily get to the place He has called you to be.

Only desperation will bring about this type of intimacy on a regular basis. Have you ever loved something or someone so much you were absolutely desperate for it or them? Usually when a man and a woman fall in love they feel this way. Nothing can keep them apart. This is how it was with my wife and I, I could not wait to get to her when I got off work. To this day, I love being in her presence and as a result we enjoy a great intimacy in our marriage. I know her, good and bad, and she knows me the same way.

The Tree of Intimacy

It is easy to see what we are desperate for in our lives. I know some men who are desperate for football, or racing, or hunting, or fishing. For me it used to be football. I played and coached high school and college football for over 13 years and I absolutely lived for it! I could not wait to get to the next practice, game or meeting. To this day, I have friends who can watch football for several hours on Saturday or Sunday, but have never even dreamed of praying or seeking God for so long a time. They wake up at 4:30am to go hunting or fishing, but have never sought God at such an hour. And yet we say we want revival. We say we are desperate for God to move in our churches and our nation. How desperate are we? How much are we seeking an intimacy with Him that will bring forth change in our world? What do we show we love by our actions and sacrifices of time? Today, just like in the Bible, He desires that we turn from our idols and return to Him!

An idol is something that takes the place of Him in our lives. What is keeping you from a life of radical devotion to God? Maybe we should consider fasting from these things. I used to think that fasting was only "real fasting" if you abstained from food. But I think sometimes that fasting from food is easier for us in our culture than fasting from many other things. What do we give our time to? How much time do you spend reading newspapers or reading emails? How long are you surfing the internet or playing video games? How about playing golf? Now, don't get me wrong, God wants us to enjoy our lives, but He is also seeking a people that will radically seek His face. What is more important to you?

If we love Him above all else, we will lovingly devote our lives to Him. It is no sacrifice to lay down your life and your self before Jesus! I assure you that He has a life filled with more pleasure and fun than you could ever imagine. I became a Christian as an adult and I remember thinking in those early days of walking with Him, things like: "Do I have to give up everything to be a Christian?" or "What will I do for fun?" You see, my whole life up to that point had been all about me. Praise God, it wasn't to long before He revealed to me how much better it is to live for Jesus than for myself. Now I get to travel all over the world and get to see Jesus touch thousands of people with His love and power. Being His servant is better than being the king of my old life any day of the week! As king of my world, I lived a life in bondage to so many things, and at best, I ruled over a huge mess! Now I get to walk side by side with the King of the Universe and watch with humility and awe as He sets His children free. Pretty good trade if you ask me!

The Veil is Torn Open

In Matthew 27 we read the account of the crucifixion of Jesus. It tells that in the moment that Jesus died on the cross or "yielded up His spirit," that "the veil of the temple was torn in two from top to bottom…" The veil in the temple was to keep the glory of God contained within the temple. The ark and the glory of God laid behind the veil in the Holy of Holies. Only the priests of Israel could enter into the presence of God. But now, with the death of Jesus on the cross, the veil was forever torn in two. What this means now, is that each and every believer in Jesus Christ, that has been bought and washed in His precious blood, can freely and boldly approach the very throne room of God almighty! We need not be afraid or nervous, but it is your birthright, as a born again child of God, to enter into His presence. Not only that, but He desires that you be there, in a place if intimacy with Him on a regular basis!

This veil is torn forever. Only you can keep yourself out of that holy place. How sad it would be to stay in the outer courts of His kingdom, when his heart is for you to be at His side. You are being summoned to the side of the King! If the President called you today and asked you to join him for a private meeting in the oval office, would you hesitate? Of course not! I am sure you would be greatly honored and hurry to make sure you were there and not a minute late. Well, the King of Kings has called you to His private chambers today. Please don't hesitate, but run to Him.

You Are Who You Hang Around

You have no doubt heard the old saying "You are who you hang around." And we all know that there is a lot of truth in that statement. We can probably all think of people in our lives that are upset

The Tree of Intimacy

and negative and sometimes these upset and negative people are drawn to each other. They may sit around and complain all day and talk about how bad their lives are. And you know what, their lives always stay bad and they become more like each other all the time!

Or maybe you can remember when you were a teenager and how you began to become exactly like all the friends you associated with. It is just a fact that we become like our environment. If you want to be a success in the business world, hang around people who are successful in business and speak confidence and optimism. If you want to be a winner, hang around winners, and if you want to be more like Jesus, spend time in His presence. As you sit and dwell in His presence, as you soak in His glory, it will rub off on you. You will begin to be transformed more and more into His image. You will also begin to take on His nature and characteristics at a quicker rate the more you are with Him. A sure fire way for success in ministry and fulfilling your divine destiny,

is to spend more and more time on your face before Him.

There is a man from South Korea that the Lord has been using to win many souls for Jesus all over the world. One characteristic of his ministry are the amazing miracles that accompany his preaching. A Russian pastor my family knows once asked Him why he believes there are so many signs and wonders that follow his ministry and he answered, "For many years I have spent eight hours a day in prayer." Time with Him enables us to be more like Him, and when we are more like Him, He can more readily use us for His purposes and glory. Are we that hungry to see God move in our lives?

The Tree And Its Fruit

Not long ago, when I had a free morning, I grabbed my Bible and went off to one of my favorite places to seek the Lord and pray. This particular morning, I was fired up. I was just in one of those moods where I had determined I was going to lay down before the Lord and not leave until He had spoke to me, until He had met with me. When I arrived, I began fully prepared to press in and stay for a long time, but to my surprise within a few minutes the Lord gave me a great revelation and when I left that morning I knew I was to write this down and share it with others. From this revelation came the small book you are reading right now.

On the wall of the prayer chapel at Regent University which is very close to my home, is a beautiful stained glass window. On the window is a large tree and on the tree there are different kinds of fruit. I was praying in desperation for God, that I might know Him more intimately and He began to show me a meaning for this tree. Before I go into this, I know that the original stained glass artist had His own meaning that went into this work of art. But this day, the Lord used it to show me something unique and new to me. Often times the beauty of a piece of art lies in its ability to speak differently to different people. How much more so when the work is inspired by a Christian artist filled with the Holy Spirit!

This day, the Lord showed me that this tree was intimacy. Our intimate relationship with God should be the center of our lives and at the center of the church just as this window was in the center of the small room I was in. This intimacy, when cultivated into a lifestyle, will produce great fruit in our lives and for our generation. The three types of fruit that I believe will be the primary forces that God will use to shake the nations and draw them unto Himself will be the fruit of love, the fruit of power, and the fruit of blessing. From our intimacy with the Father will come such love and power as the world has never seen and will only be able to be explained as the power of God Himself. This love, power, and blessing will be undeniable. From this tree of intimacy will come these three fruits which are the essence of His glory. And when His glory comes upon the church, we will not have to advertise it, the world will see it! This tree of intimacy has been talked about in this chapter. The rest of our book will now focus on the fruits that we can expect from this new level of intimacy that God is calling us to. Let's get into the fruit!

Part Two

The Fruit of Love

God is Love

One day recently I was sitting on the beach near my home in Virginia. Although I have lived in close proximity to the Atlantic Ocean all of my life, it is only in recent years that I have really began to appreciate it. Sitting there on the beach, watching the waves crash against the sandy shore, my thoughts quickly drifted to the awesome God that created this great sea. The sheer power of the ocean is remarkable. Within its depths live millions of species of life and within its waves lies the power to wash away entire villages and civilizations. Pondering these things, I felt I heard the Lord say inside my head "You can hear My voice in those waves if you listen." Surely the waves of the ocean and all of His creation carry the voice of God. Creation speaks to us of the love of God, that He created all this for His children. How in the world did man's noise ever drown out the voice of God's love in His creation around us?

The Bible tells us that "God is love."[10] Now, since we were created in the image of God, we can then say that we were created by God in love, to be loved, and to also give love. We, as Christians, should naturally be loving people, but for some reason, this is not always the case. Why is this? After all, aren't we filled with the Holy Spirit? An outsider or unbeliever looks at the church as a whole and sees a big mess. We fight over our sometimes petty differences. We publicly rebuke our brothers and sisters who see things slightly different than we do. Now, I am not talking about heresy or major theological truths here, just small, little theological or even cultural differences. Our churches in America are still largely segregated. Yet Jesus says "By this all men will know that you are my disciples, if you have love for one another."[11]

Where is the love that stands in sharp contrast to the rest of the world? Where is the love that the world will see and know that we are His disciples? The love that will make them say, "Wow! What is this! This has got to be for real!" Well, that extreme and radical love is in existence today. It is evident in the lives and ministries of the few believers who have experienced a personal revelation of the love of the Father. We must be zealous for the things of God. We must earnestly desire this type of love in our lives.

This love that we need comes only from daily intimacy with God. Time in His presence, crying out desperately to Him always results in a revelation of His awesome, unconditional love for us and for this world. God is longing to share this love with us and for us to then share it with the world. This tree of intimacy in the church is to first feed the church with the fruit of His love and the fruit of His power and then the world will come running when they see this amazing fruit.

God has chosen to reveal His glory to the earth through the church. Since the beginning, God has revealed Himself to the world through man. Remember, Adam was created in His image. So much so, I believe that when the rest of creation saw Adam in the garden they saw the very image or a reflection of God. I think we have fallen into a way of thinking in the church that says we need to pray for God to do everything for us, when He wants to use us to do it!

A great example of this is given to us in Mark chapter 4. Here we read of the disciples and Jesus in the boat during a storm. The storm was raging around them and the tiny boat that they were in. Scared to death, the disciples awoke Jesus and said "Teacher, do you not care that we are perishing?" Upon being awakened, Jesus stilled the storm with His words "Hush, be still." It was a great miracle that Jesus could command even the winds and the seas. Then, what did Jesus do when everything was calm? He rebuked His disciples by saying "Why are you afraid? Do you still have no faith?"[12] It is evident by this passage that Jesus wanted His disciples to not be afraid, to not just cry out to Him with all of their problems expecting Him to do it without them. He wanted them to have the faith necessary to still the storm. He can do it alone, but He has chosen from the beginning of time to work through us. Today, God wants His church to carry out His will on earth! God's desire is to lavish the earth with His love by using us to do it!

But we cannot even hope to affect the world with the love of Jesus Christ unless we first have a personal encounter with the Father's great love ourselves. Here is an illustration. Imagine you are a glass and the love of God is water. God stands over us and pours that water into us and fills us with as much water as we ask for. The one who keeps asking for more, continues to receive more until they begin to overflow to the others around them. It will not be long before everything around them is soaking wet. This is what the Lord wants. He wants to fill us with His love until we overflow uncontrollably and saturate the world around us. This must begin in the church. The hard part is we are obviously not yet full and few of us know how much is available to us.

God is looking for empty vessels to fill with His love! It is all available to you today. Cry out to Him, for Him to saturate you in His love, to fill you to a point of running over and then just rest in it for a while. Let Him soak you in His love. Now, I want you to think about something with me for a moment. If God is love, and we are to be transformed by the renewing of our mind, what are we to be transformed more and more into? We are to be transformed into His image, which is at its very core love. If you are a Christian, God is doing a work in you today. From the moment you accepted Him into your heart, He has been transforming you as you allow Him. He wants to take you and I, who for the most part are incapable of true, unconditional, undeserved, love and transform us into a reflection of His divine self. We are being transformed by the renewing of our minds and Spirits into a vessel that contains a full measure of the love of almighty God Himself! This is His desire for you! So again, I ask you today to cry out for this love in your life!

Without Love We Have Nothing

The New Testament itself is totally built around love. The gospels of Matthew, Mark, Luke, and John all focus on the greatest act of love in the history of the Universe. Namely, that which is described in John 3:16. *"For God so loved the world that He gave His only begotten Son, that whosoever believes in Him shall not perish, but have everlasting life."*

The gospel message is hands down the greatest love story there is. The Cross is the key event in the history of the world and the greatest act of love ever seen. So great, that it has forever changed the course of the life of every man and woman before or since.

When most of us think about love in Scripture, we think of 1 Corinthians 13. Let's just look at one verse of this passage, verse 2. "If I have the gift of prophecy, and know all the mysteries and all knowledge and if I have all faith, so as to remove mountains, but do not have love, I am nothing." This passage reveals so much to us about the importance of love in the kingdom of God as a whole. It takes the gifts that many of us feel are the most important or at least essential for a victorious life in God's kingdom, and says to us that even with these great gifts, that without love we have nothing! Great faith is useless unless it is backed by love, all the gifts of the Spirit are useless without love. You see everything in the kingdom hinges on the "key" element. If there is a periodic table of elements in the spiritual realm, the biggest and baddest of all the elements is without a doubt, love.

That said, love like this, love that makes people take notice, changes lives, moves mountains, and shakes cities and nations for God's glory, comes only from time spent on your knees or your face in the presence of almighty God. We find excuses today for lack of time in His presence. And yet we still wish we had more love in our life. I've had people ask me things like this "Do I need to get on my knees to pray?" or "God knows we are busy in our society so isn't 15 minutes of prayer a day good enough?" 15 minutes of prayer a day is a great place to begin, but let's go back to what we said earlier, you can have as much of God in your life as you want. If you want a life filled with the supernatural manifestation of God, I encourage you to spend every minute you can spare crying out for Him and a revelation of His all encompassing love. And if you really believe He is God Almighty, and you ever see a glimpse of His glory, you won't have to ask about getting on your knees to pray, you will fall on your knees and on your face pretty quick. If He is truly our everything, why can't we get on our knees or on our faces and cry out to Him? If He is God, why are satisfied sitting and praying for 15 minutes when we are in the presence of the Almighty!

I had a revelation once during a time of prayer. I was sitting on a bed praying when I heard the Lord say, "Get on you knees and take off your shoes, for you are on Holy Ground." I believe the Lord was saying to me that He desired me to understand how precious His presence is. So often we take it for granted. How many men and women in the Old Testament would have given anything for five minutes of what we have access to every day? Because of the love of God and the cross, we can now meet with Him anytime! If we had a free lifetime membership to the gym, we would probably use it every day. Well, how much more valuable is a free lifetime membership into the Holy of Holies!

Increasing Our Capacity

The Father loves His children and He is tired of seeing us struggle with our pasts, memories, and things that He has paid such a high price for already. The Son has set you free! The death of Jesus on the cross paid for it all! His great love has set you free from all addictions, abuse, fear, guilt, bitterness, unforgiveness, generational curses, sickness, disease, pornography, occult involvement, or whatever else the enemy is using to hold you back from God's plan for your life.

Chances are you have struggled with one or more of the above mentioned problems in your life. We all have. Satan, the enemy, uses your hurts, and your guilt, and shame, and literally holds you hostage from experiencing the fullness of God's will for you. Satan will tell you that you are alone and that you are the only one facing such difficulties. He will tell you that you are undeserving of the Fathers love. I want you to know that there is nothing that you can do that will make God love you any more or any less. God has forgiven you, and He wants you to forgive yourself. If something bad happened to you in the past, Jesus was right there with you, you were not alone then, and if you will run to Him today, He is waiting with open arms to heal you totally. His love is always the same. It is always unconditional and undeserved. It is a gift.

As a church and individually, it is essential that we daily position ourselves to receive God's love. God is an extravagant God. Nothing He has created is short of a masterpiece, including His children. God does all things extravagantly. He is almighty God! When He blesses He blesses abundantly. His Word tells us that He came that we might have life and have it more abundantly.[13] When He pours His love upon a church that is earnestly seeking and desiring Him, He does not hold back! He lavishes it upon us! When we love a little, He loves a lot, and when we ask for more of His love, it comes in waves that are in proportion to our capacity to receive it.

In today's church we seem to have a capacity problem. I honestly believe God is pouring out His Spirit upon all flesh, but only in the amount that we can handle. This is true with His power and blessing, which we will cover in later chapters, and with His love. To be filled by God's love, we must first be totally empty. I heard the famous German evangelist Rheinhard Bonnke use the following illustration once that explains this well. He said that our lives are like a large house with many rooms. When we ask Jesus into our lives to be our Lord and savior, we give over almost every room to be filled by His Spirit and love. But we also usually keep a few doors locked up. We hold onto these rooms that remain from our old life before Christ as though the pleasure they give us could somehow be better than the great and wonderful things the Lord wants to fill us with! Think about that! For some it is hidden sin, for some it is old habits or ways of thinking, for some others still it is negative attitudes. We may say, "This is just who I am." Or "This is just a part of me." That is just a lie the enemy wants you to believe.

Whatever it may be in our own lives, we need to give it to Him. He wants it all. He desires access to every area of our lives. Only when we are full of His love can we ever hope to run over and affect the world around us.

The time has come for the church to make room for the glory of the Lord in our midst. We need to be empty so He can use us to our full potential. A car with only a little fuel can go only a small distance. A church with only a little love can only be used at a fraction of our full potential in Christ. I have heard it said that we are like a 75watt light bulb screwed into a million volt super transformer. If God were to release His love into the church at full measure we would explode! However, if we will empty ourselves one at a time before Him, He will fill us fully, one by one. As each church is filled with vessels that are full of His extravagant love, this nation and this world will be affected. Revival will come. But we must understand that love like this, and a revelation of it, comes only through times of intimacy with Him. It is in these intimate moments that we are filled with His essence.

This love in our lives is birthed by extreme passion for the Father. You have heard it said that "Without vision the people perish." Revivalist Leonard Ravenhill wrote in His classic *Why Revival Tarries*, "Where there is no passion the church perishes, even though it be full to the doors."[14] The church is in danger today. The enemy can not stop the church, but He can deceive us into believing that we are "successful," particularly if our attendance is high and our churches are full. Some disguise and alter the gospel message and thus spend years apologizing for a gospel that as it is *"is the power of God unto salvation."* Others go through the motions with many wonderful programs, but a close examination reveals more of a passion to "be successful" or to "grow" than a passion for our Father.

Pastors greet each other in some circles by saying "How many are you running on Sundays?" We may ask our friends "How many people do you have in your church?" Like the number of people meeting is the defining factor in anything in the kingdom. God is looking for devotion, passion, and cries of longing from His children. Of course, more is better, it is God's will for the church to grow, and we want the halls of heaven full, but give me two people sold out for Jesus over a thousand in a dead church any day of the week! I have been in meetings from 10,000 people to 10 people and God always responds to hunger for Him, faith, and expectancy. Time and experience are teaching me that faith and expectancy for God to move come from hunger, desperation and passion for Him! What we need are mega churches sold out and burning white hot for Jesus!

Are we really hungry for Him! Are we desperate for His love? Sometimes we see young lovers like Romeo and Juliet commit suicide over the love they have for each other. Do we love Jesus so much that we will do anything to be with Him? Unlike those young lovers who sometimes find a partner who does not share their great love, we always have a Father who is desperate for us as well. As much as you need and want an intimate relationship with Him, He wants one with you!

His Love Brings Joy and Gladness

As Christians, we are called to be a joyful and happy people. Chances are though, you know or have met, quite a few "grumpy" Christians. Some of us find it easy to complain and murmur over the least little things in our lives. Meanwhile, the God of all creation desires to be our closest friend and confidant. You have a Bible full of tremendous promises that assure His love, provision and care in every area of your life. Yet, still we often complain. Scripture surely shows us that it is God's will for us to live lives full of joy and gladness. With the pressures and stresses of our modern lives how can this be possible? The only way is through a personal encounter with the love of Jesus every day. A day out of the Lord's presence and you will quickly begin to lose your joy. It does not take long outside of His presence before we can find ourselves in some pretty scary places.

From time to time, David found himself in some scary places in his life too, but as we know, he maintained a closeness to the lord that serves to this day as a great example. For all his faults, adultery, murder, etc., David sought the face of God like no other, and as a result, he was forever lifted up as God called him "a man after His

The Tree of Intimacy

own heart." There is a passage from Psalm 16 that David penned, that speaks loudly today to us concerning God's presence and the joy that is sure to follow. Verses 8-11 read:

"I have set the Lord continually before me; because He is at my right hand, I will not be shaken. Therefore my heart is glad and my glory rejoices; my flesh also will dwell securely. For You will not abandon my soul to Sheol; nor will you allow your Holy One to undergo decay. You will make known to me the path of life; in Your presence is fullness of joy; in your right hand there are pleasures forever."

David starts out by saying he has "set the Lord continually before me" meaning that he is constantly seeking God's presence. He has invited the Lord into every minute of his life. He goes on to say that the Lord is his "right hand" and he "will not be shaken." What he is telling us is that God is his protector and sustainer in all things. With God as his protector and sustainer, David can boldly say that he "will not be shaken." Therefore, he continues by saying "my heart is glad." David's "heart is glad" because he is confident in the reality that he is dwelling in God's presence. David then writes "You will make known to me the path of life" As the king spends time with God, God has been faithful to lead him in the way he was meant to go.

Now we come to our key part of this passage. David writes " in your presence is fullness of joy; in your right hand there are pleasures forever." David lived a life pursuing a relationship with God, and he knew that in God's presence, where all the above things are realized, joy abounds above all else. In times of intimacy, God reveals Himself to His beloved. Remember, that God is love, and from a revelation of that love, there can only be a manifestation of joy in our lives.

If our car is running badly, we usually would go to a mechanic and ask him to perform a diagnostic evaluation on it to see what is wrong. Sometimes we need to do a similar check up on ourselves. When you meet with God regularly, you cannot help but be changed by His love and filled with a great joy that oozes from every pore of your body. So, if you find yourself not full of joy, or as we sometimes say "down in the dumps," there is a disconnect somewhere. For too long, as a church, it seems we have been satisfied with just being saved. God has so much more for us! If we are with Him daily, if we are bringing Him into every moment, His joy will be all over us. If it is not, we need to run to Him. His promise is that we will always find Him there waiting.

The Father's Love Letter

The following "love letter" is compiled from many verses from Genesis to Revelation. I have found nothing better that shows God's heart for His children. As you read this letter, please take time to consider the significance of all these promises of love from God. In the future, in times of prayer, use these verses to meditate on God's amazing love, goodness and character. Through those times, I know He will share much more insight and revelation into His wonderful heart for you, and for the world around you. From these promises, your view of yourself will be changed, and only when you understand who you really are, and how He loves you, can our Father use us to show His love to our families, communities, and the world. This letter is from your Father to you.

> My Child…
> You may not know Me, but I know everything about you…
>   Psalm 139:1
> I know you when you sit down and when you rise up…
>   Psalm 139:2
> Even the very hairs on your head are numbered…
>   Matthew 10:29-31
> For you were made in my image… Genesis 1:27
> In Me you live and move and have your being… Acts 17:28
> For You are My offspring… Acts 17:28
> I knew you even before you were conceived… Jeremiah 1:4-5
> I chose you when I planned creation… Ephesians 1:11-12
> You were not a mistake, for all your days are written in my
>   book… Psalm 139:15-16

I determined the exact time of your birth and where you would
   live... Acts 17:26
You are fearfully and wonderfully made... Psalm 139:14
I knit you together in your mother's womb... Psalm 139:13
And brought you fort on the day you were born...Psalm 71:6
I have been misrepresented by those who don't know me...
   John 8:41-44
I am not distant and angry, but am the complete expression of
   love... 1 John 4:16
And it is My desire is to lavish my love on you... 1 John 3:1
Simply because you are my child and I am your father...
   1 John 3:1
I offer you more than your earthly father ever could...
   Matthew 7:11
For I am the perfect Father... Matthew 5:48
Every good gift that you receive comes from My hand...
   James 1:17
For I am your provider, and I meet all your needs...
   Matthew 6:31-33
My plan for your future has always been filled with hope...
   Jeremiah 29:11
Because I love you with an everlasting love... Jeremiah 31:3
My thoughts toward you are as countless as the sand on the
   seashore... Psalm 139:17-18
And I rejoice over you with singing... Zephaniah 3:17
I will never stop doing good to you... Jeremiah 32:40
For you are my treasured possession... Exodus 19:5
I desire to establish you with all My heart and all My soul...
   Jeremiah 32:41
And I want to show you great and marvelous things...
   Jeremiah 33:3
If you seek me with all your heart, you will find Me...
   Deuteronomy 4:29
Delight in Me, and I will give you the desires of your heart...
   Psalm 37:4
For it is I who gave you those desires... Philippians 2:13
I am able to do more for you than you could possibly imagine...

Ephesians 3:20
For I am your greatest encourager... 2 Thessalonians 2:16-17
I am also the Father who comforts you in all you troubles...
   2Corinthians 1:3-4
When you are brokenhearted, I am close to you... Psalm 34:18
As a shepherd carries a lamb, I have carried you close to my
   heart...Isaiah 40:11
One day I will wipe away every tear from your eyes...
   Revelation 21:3-4
And I'll take away all the pain you have suffered on this
   earth...Revelation 21:3-4
I am your Father, and I love you even as I love My Son,
   Jesus... John 17:23
For in Jesus, My love for you is revealed... John 17:26
He is the exact representation of My being... Hebrews 1:3
He came to demonstrate that I am for you, not against you...
   Romans 8:31
And to tell you that I am not counting your sins...
   2 Corinthians 5:18-19
Jesus died so that you and I could be reconciled...
   2 Corinthians 5:18-19
His death was the ultimate expression of My love for you...
   1 John 4:10
I gave up everything that I might regain your love...
   Romans 8:31-32
If you receive the gift of My Son, Jesus, you receive Me...
   1 John 2:23
And nothing will ever separate you from My love again...
   Romans 8:38-39
Come home, and I'll throw the biggest party heaven has ever
   seen... Luke 15:7
I have always been Father and will always be Father...
   Ephesians 3:14-15
My question is... Will you be My child? ... John 1:12-13
I am waiting for you... Luke 15;11-32
Love, Your Dad, Almighty God[15]

Part Three

The Fruit of Power

Love Produces Power

The gospel is called in Romans 1:16 "the power of God...." Everywhere the gospel went forth in the New Testament record, there were always displays of divine power or signs and wonders that confirmed the gospel message. When Jesus ministered on the earth we easily see that power was definitely a characteristic of His ministry. You cannot separate the power of the Holy Spirit from the gospel. They go hand in hand. Without the power of the Holy Spirit you are not preaching the full gospel of Jesus Christ. For Jesus is risen and He is a living God!

As I mentioned in the introduction to this book, the anointing of power that the Lord wants to manifest in this generation, can only come about when we have a revelation of His love in our lives and for the world around us. We need to know Him intimately before we can flow in the power and anointing He has for us. When you know His love for you, you begin to understand His great love for all people. After all, He came that all might know Him, that all might be saved. The seven sons of Sceva in Acts 19:14 tried to work wonders and drive out demons in the name of Jesus without knowing Him and look what happened to them!

Intimacy with God brings love and love produces power. They build on each other. The love of God revealed to us transforms our senses. We begin to see with eyes of compassion, the very eyes of Christ. Pray daily for these eyes. That you might see all things and people as He does. Earlier, I shared of how in Brazil when I prayed for the sick and oppressed with genuine love in my heart, there was a huge difference in the manifestation of God's power in the service. When I looked them in the eyes, I felt in my heart the love of Christ. That love moved me to anger at the enemy and boldness to speak God's promises of healing over their lives. I extended my hand, and He extended His because my heart was transformed, my eyes were transformed, and my hands became his instruments of healing and love. In the church, the world will soon see what I call the divine dichotomy. Like Jesus we will wield the love and power of God with boldness and confidence. He is the Lion and the Lamb. Only God can put the lion and the lamb together in us in such a way that the world will take notice.

Like intimacy, many have mistakenly thought that such manifestations of God's power could be expected only in the lives of the five-fold ministers: apostles, prophets, evangelists, pastors or teachers. I want to spend the remaining portion of this section of the book sharing how signs and wonders are to be expected in the life of all believers.

A Lesson In Authority: God Wants to Use You!

In the Bible, authority plays a very prominent role. In the New Testament we can easily see a definite progression of divine authority. To begin, all authority in the universe originates with God the Father. We then see in scripture that all authority was passed on to Jesus the Son. In Matthew 28:18 Jesus says, *"All authority has been given to Me in heaven and on earth."* Without a doubt, the authority of Jesus was readily seen through the powerful works that He did under the anointing of the Holy Spirit.

It is worth noting that Jesus never began His earthly ministry until He was anointed by the Holy Spirit at His baptism in the

The Tree of Intimacy

Jordan by John. Then, after a time of testing and temptation in the wilderness, He began to minister under the most powerful anointing of the Holy Spirit that the World had ever witnessed.

This powerful anointing rested upon Jesus throughout His remaining days on this earth and when the time was appropriate, this power was entrusted to His beloved disciples. In Matthew 10:1,7-8 we read, *"Jesus summoned His twelve disciples and gave them authority over unclean spirits, to cast them out, and to heal every kind of disease and every kind of sickness...* "And as you go, preach, saying, 'The kingdom of heaven is at hand.' "Heal the sick, raise the dead, cleanse the lepers, cast out demons. Freely you received, freely give." Jesus clearly stated that the disciples were going out armed with the authority or power to carry out that which they had been sent out to do. Jesus armed them with what was necessary to get the job done. Just as Jesus went about "doing good and healing all those who were oppressed by the devil" as shown in Acts 10:38, so now are we his disciples to go and do the same.

The good news is that this transfer of divine power and authority did not stop with the original twelve Apostles. In Luke 10 Jesus *"appointed seventy others, and sent them in pairs ahead of Him...and heal those who are sick, and say to them, 'The kingdom of God has come near to you.'* "Behold, I have given you authority to tread on serpents and scorpions, and over all the power of the enemy, and nothing will injure you."

This passage is amazing for several reasons. Of note is the fact that Jesus bestowed this authority so freely on such a large group of followers. This was not for the "inner circle" of beloved disciples. These were most likely just a group of those who were willing to be sent. Another astounding fact about this event is that the text clearly reads that authority was given *"over all the power of the enemy...."* Jesus did not just bestow power in little spurts or at levels just enough to empress the average townspeople, rather He freely gave this power and authority in a great amount.

What makes this power transfer all the more monumental in importance is that Jesus was not content to let this authority and power over the enemy die with these men of the first century. The kingdom was now at hand! At the end of the Gospel of Mark, Jesus gives a charge and commission to all who would become believers throughout the ages.[16] All who know Him as Lord would be heirs to this wonderful promise.

> *"Go into all the world and preach the gospel to all creation. He who has believed and been baptized shall be saved; but he who has disbelieved shall be condemned. These signs **will** accompany **those** who have believed: in my name they will cast out demons, they will speak with new tongues; they will pick up serpents, and if they drink any deadly poison, it will not hurt them; they will lay hands on the sick, and they will recover." "And they went out and preached everywhere, while the Lord worked with them, and confirmed the word by the signs that followed."* (Mk. 16:15-18,20)

We as believers are called to go out and share the good news of Jesus Christ. Most of us have little problem with that part of the Great Commission. Where the problem lies is where we have to have a greater faith. The problem is that most of us do not believe *we* have *any* authority over the enemy. If we do, we sure aren't acting like it. It seems we believe that Jesus has power, and that Satan has power. We have no problem even believing that Jesus has more power and even "all" power over the enemy.

I believe the Lord's question to the church today is this, Why have you chosen to not believe that I have given all power and authority unto *you*?! The Word of God speaks clearly as we have seen in Scripture in the previous paragraphs. He has given us all authority and power over the enemy. When we go to work, to school, to the store, or to the nations, He has sent us out with the very anointing of the Holy Spirit that He ministered under. The same Holy Spirit that rose Jesus from the dead, the same Holy Spirit that descended upon Him in the Jordan, is the same Holy Spirit that is available to us as Christians today! The world is desperately waiting for a church that is like Jesus, that is doing His works, that is *"healing all those who are oppressed by the devil."* This world and I would say this 21st century church is greatly oppressed.

Let us awaken and realize that we are in the midst of a great war. The victory has been won by Jesus and the finished work of the cross. Satan is defeated. But, we must now fight the battles that lay between today and the second coming of the Lord. . Jesus goes before us, but we must still fight. He has chosen to use us.

A similar example of such a war can be seen in the Old Testament book of Joshua. Joshua and the Israelites had been assured victory. They know that God's will is for them to have the Land. He has given it to them. Yet they must still go in and fight the present rulers and inhabitants. They go armed with the power and favor of God Himself, but they still must go. We too are armed, like no other army in the history of the world. Even the newest believer in the Lord is arrayed with weapons more powerful than anything the enemy has in his camp.[17] Let's wake up and see that the time has come to fight! The battle is for the harvest of the souls of the earth. God is moving today like never before. More people are coming to know the Lord Jesus than ever before and God is truly pouring out His Spirit upon all flesh. The great end time harvest of God is upon us! And guess what? You have a part to play!

A Story Of Men With No Names

One day in 2002, I heard David Cartledge of Australia preach a message on the following passage of scripture and it changed my life and ministry forever. It is such an important teaching, that I want to include it here for as many people as possible to learn from. I think it is that essential a message for our times.

There is an amazing and often overlooked passage of scripture dealing with the believer going about doing the works of Jesus that can be found in the book of Acts. In chapter 10, we read the account of Cornelius the centurion (a gentile) who has a vision of an angel of God that tells him to send for Peter. Peter, of course, has his own divine visitation where God tells him to go with the men that Cornelius has sent.

Peter's divine visitation also included a vision in which God had told him that he "should not call any man unholy or unclean." At this time in the history of the early church it was believed that the good news of Jesus Christ was intended for Jews alone. Jesus was in fact the promised Messiah of God's chosen people. So this revelation was destined to become monumental in significance to the day-to-day operations of all believers and ones sent to witness for Christ.

Peter, full of the boldness that follows a visit of this nature, bucked tradition and rightly chose to walk in obedience to God. He went with the men to the home of Cornelius and shared the gospel message with all who were there in his household. The text then tells us that while he was speaking to them the "Holy Spirit fell upon all those who were listening to the message."The Spirit was being poured out on the gentiles as well! The gospel and the accompanying gifts of the Holy Spirit were indeed for everybody! The seed of Abraham was indeed brining salvation to all men.

Now, we get to the good part of the story and the part that is essential to the purpose of this book. In chapter 11 the apostles and the believers in Judea and Jerusalem heard that the gentiles had received the message of the gospel. Needless to say, tradition and religiosity had already set in the early church! They were not pleased or rejoicing in the least at the actions of Peter. One would think that they would have been excited and overcome with joy at the news that the Spirit was indeed being poured out upon all flesh as prophesied by Joel, but instead they reprimanded Peter. Very nastily they said, "You went to uncircumcised men..."They were shocked and effectively said, "How could you!" How could Peter, one chosen by Jesus Himself, share the Word of God with such unclean men?

In his defense Peter recounted the supernatural events and basically stated that he had acted in obedience to God Himself, and when he did, God showed up in a big way and poured out His Spirit upon all who were there. This was evident by the fact that Scripture says that the circumcised who were present with Peter heard them "speaking with tongues and exalting God" Many times when someone today gets in a bit of trouble we hear them say, "The devil made me do it!" On the contrary, Peter says, "God made me do it!" Really, what was he to do?

When Peter finished his story, the apostles and believers in

Jerusalem were satisfied that this was indeed the Lord's will and "glorified God, saying, "Well then, God has granted to the gentiles also the repentance that leads to life."

But the very next verse, (v.19) shows how strong the hold of tradition and religiosity can be on the hearts and minds of men. "So then those who were scattered because of the persecution that occurred in connection with Stephen made their way to Phonecia and Cyprus and Antioch, speaking the word to no one except Jews alone." The church at large was still only preaching to Jews! Change is always so hard, and when confronted with new truth, men and women will often react with fear and anger that results from pride and the trappings of tradition.

Praise be to God that this spirit of tradition and religion would and could never thwart the will of God for His church! For in v.20, we now see new men who are raised up by God to preach the good news to all men. What is most striking and interesting in this verse is that the names of these men used so mightily by God are never given in scripture. They were not the famous apostles of Jerusalem. They were not "superstars" of the church who would be known to all for generations. The text says plainly that they were just, "men of Cyprus and Cyrene, who came to Antioch and began speaking to the Greeks also... And the hand of the Lord was with them, and a large number who believed turned toward the Lord."

Whenever the phrase "the hand of the Lord..." was used in Scripture in this way it always refers to the supernatural, wonder-working power of God. Therefore, these were ordinary believers who simply obeyed the Lord and went out boldly preaching Jesus and the Lord confirmed His word and the gospel with signs following. I would add here that the "hand of the Lord" was with them in such a way that (v.26) adds that "the disciples were first called Christians in Antioch."[18]

It is of great importance to know that the word we translate Christ is the Greek word "*Christos*" which means, "anointed one." Literally, the word Christian means "one who is like the anointed one" or "a follower of the anointed." Those of the Greek world knew this and that is why, I believe they were first called Christians here. Here these men of Cyprus and Cyrene demonstrated the anointing of the Lord in such a way that they were immediately called Christians by the populace. The anointing was that evident upon these men. They believed Jesus when He said to go forth and preach the good news and that they could be assured that all authority and power would be with them as they did. They knew that the Holy Spirit of the Living God was with them![19]

I believe that God is shedding new light on this passage today to awaken you, the believers of this generation to the truth that God wants to use you to bring to fulfillment His end-time plan and harvest and to do the works of Jesus in this world. There is a fresh sense of urgency in the church. Do not listen to the lies of the enemy that say that God doesn't move in supernatural ways in the world today. Not only does God want to unleash his miraculous power on this earth like never before, but also He desires to use you, His children to do it! Jesus walked constantly in the anointing of the Holy Spirit and so can you!

As Jesus was about the Father's business, so should we be. When we are connected to Him through times of intimacy, we know His heart, we know His will, we know His business, if you will. It is the family business and we are heirs to it. The family business is the proclamation of the gospel of the kingdom. It is to be proclaimed with all the love and power of heaven behind it. We can travel all over the world and preach the gospel, but without a revelation of the Father's heart we are just spouting off words. Without love in our hearts, we are just one of a million other incessant ramblers vying for the attention of the masses. Without His love behind it, without His power behind it, it is not the gospel.

Communion and Warfare

Claudio Freidzon, in his book *Treasure in Jars of Clay*, wrote the following about Jesus' will for all of His disciples as given in Mark 3:14-15

> *"When Jesus called His disciples, He had two purposes in mind. That is Jesus called them to have intimate communion with Him, but He also sent them to the battlefield to*

preach with authority and to defeat the devil.
"This double purpose is still valid for us today. The potter keeps on shaping us to make us into vessels of the sanctuary, jars that serve Him in worship and close communion. But He also wants to take you to the battlefield in order to win the victory.[20]

What an awesome insight into God's plan for the church. He has created us for communion with Him, to be on an intimate level with Him, and He also has plans to use us on the battlefield of faith. One who spends time with the Lord is unbeatable. God's anointed knows no defeat!

Paul understood this, and He was ready to go anywhere and anytime the Lord would send Him. I believe that is why God used Him so greatly to spread the gospel to the gentiles. He was connected to God through times of prayer and intimacy, and then when God directed, He obeyed and went. For instance, when the Lord revealed Paul was to go to Macedonia in a dream, Paul went. He did not hesitate. Smith Wigglesworth wrote of how he envied Paul's readiness to serve God boldly when he said "I want to ever be in Paul's position – that at any time, even at midnight, in the face of anything, even death itself, God may be able to manifest His power and to do what He wants to do through me."[21] Wigglesworth, like Paul, was used greatly for God's glory, because he too spent huge amounts of time seeking God's face, will, and direction and then He went out and acted on what the Lord had revealed in those times of intimacy.

Jesus our Divine Model

As Christians, we are to seek to be more and more like our Lord. We should of course pray that we take on more of His likeness as He leads us on our daily journey with Him. Sadly and mistakenly in the church, we too often look to other Christians as the model of godly behavior. Now, don't get me wrong, there are many wonderful Christian role models in the church, and we would do well to learn a great deal from them, and incorporate many of their habits and disciplines in our lives, but there is no model of how to live the Christian life that compares to Christ Himself. We need only to look to Him. We all know the popular Christian slogan that is emblazoned on so many t-shirts and pendants today, "What would Jesus do?." Well, I would ask you to consider for a moment, this question, "What *did* Jesus do?" and if I may ask another, "What is He still doing today?" Let us fix our eyes on Him! Let us behold Him, that we might be changed!

First, let us look at what Jesus did, according to what we have handed down to us in the Word of God. One passage we have already mentioned is Acts 10:38 " *You know of Jesus of Nazareth, how God anointed Him with the Holy Spirit and with power, and how He went about doing good and healing all who were oppressed by the devil for God was with Him.*" Here we see that He was anointed by the Holy Spirit and with power. Now we see an interesting progression in His actions. He was first anointed and then He went about doing good and healing all those oppressed by the devil. The anointing and the power came and then Jesus, being equipped for His mission, went about both doing good and healing the oppressed.

Another excellent scripture that gives a great deal of insight into Jesus' earthly ministry is Matthew 4:23. This scripture is describing the ministry of our Lord in Galilee. It reads, "*Jesus was going throughout all Galilee, teaching in the synagogues and proclaiming the gospel of the kingdom, and healing every kind of disease and every kind of sickness among the people.*" This passage points out what many have termed the three-fold ministry of Jesus. The three facets pointed out here are teaching, proclaiming, and healing. Jesus taught those around Him. He proclaimed the good news that the kingdom of heaven was at hand! Things had changed! It also said that Jesus healed. Jesus healed many in His earthly ministry, but we must point out that Jesus did not heal all the sick in Jerusalem or Judea. For instance, many were at the pool of Bethsaida, but Jesus went to only one. This is important because many who claim that God does not use Christians to heal the sick today say that if Christians did have the gift of healing, why aren't they spending all day in the hospital healing every sick person in the world. I would say to them that even Jesus did not heal every sick person He encountered. God is God and we are not. He is sovereign. His ways are not ours and we will never, ever, have all the answers. But we are called to have faith. We know it is His will that the sick would be healed and we as His followers must obey Him out of love. We must act accordingly in faith.

From these two passages we may gather that Jesus was first anointed with the Spirit and power, then went about doing good, healed those who were oppressed by the devil, taught, proclaimed and healed those with both diseases and sicknesses. Well, that is a lot, but there was still more to the earthly ministry of Christ.

The next passage we must study is extremely crucial, because the gospel account (Luke 4) shows Jesus Himself using this verse to describe His ministry and life. The passage is Luke 4:18-19 and reads,

> *"The Spirit of the Lord is upon me, because He anointed Me to preach the gospel to the poor. He has sent me to proclaim release to the captives, and recovery of sight to the blind, to set free those who are oppressed, to proclaim the favorable year of the Lord..."*

Here again, even Jesus Himself stresses the anointing of the Holy Spirit. Noted theologian J. Rodman Williams states regarding this passage, "It is in this passage that the Spirit and the anointing are most clearly connected: the Coming One (Jesus) will carry out His mission through the anointing of the Holy Spirit."[22] There is a purpose for this supernatural anointing. Jesus said that the Spirit had anointed Him to bring good news to the afflicted, (some translations render "afflicted" as "poor") to bind up the broken hearted, to proclaim liberty to the captives, freedom to the prisoners, and to proclaim the favorable year of the Lord.

What exactly does all this mean? What was Jesus saying when He read this scripture, and made known to the crowd, that He was the fulfillment of this prophecy? I think it would be best to look at each of these above purposes individually. Each one of these is essential to our understanding of the ministry of the Lord and what

He would have His church and every individual believer do today.

The Anointing

The first thing we see in this scripture is that Jesus was anointed by the Holy Spirit. He said that the "Spirit of the Lord God" was upon Him. We must understand that Jesus did not begin His earthly ministry until the Holy Spirit descended upon Him at His baptism in the Jordan by John. Then, and only then, did Jesus begin His earthly ministry.

We too must know that if we attempt to undertake our calling without the anointing of the Lord we are in for a hard road. Every work that does not have God's anointed signature upon it is as good as dead. The Word tells us plainly that "it is not by might, nor by power, but by the Holy Spirit." Jesus walked constantly in the anointing and so can we. Make no mistake, the Lord wants to fill us with His power. He is not hiding from you, nor does He want to withhold from you any good thing. He desperately wants us to minister in His anointing so He can pour out His love, blessing, healing, compassion, mercy, and grace all over the world. When we are anointed by Him, we are empowered to move and walk in the Spirit, and do the works of Jesus Christ. Without it, we merely do the works of men. We may have the best intentions, but we will ultimately be laboring in the flesh. We will at best only scratch the surface of what the Lord has for us.

So, I want to take this opportunity to encourage you to pray that the Lord will pour out His Spirit upon you in a new way. If you are not baptized in the Holy Spirit pray to receive this baptism now. Open yourself up to God and allow Him to fill you. It is my sincere and earnest prayer that you would continually walk in the anointing of His Spirit. Remember this, if you give Him everything, if you live for Him alone, if you hunger and thirst for Him, He will anoint you, He will direct you, and He will use you to do great and mighty things for His kingdom!

Bringing The Gospel To The Afflicted or Poor

For what reason did Jesus say He was anointed? In other words, "What was He to do?" Well, the first purpose He gives in this passage is to "preach the gospel to the poor…" Another similar verse that comes to mind is (Mt. 9:12) where Jesus is responding to the accusations of the Pharisees by saying "It is not those who are healthy who need a physician, but those who are sick."

Going against the ways of the world, Jesus is saying that this "gospel" or "good news" is for the poor, the afflicted, the outcast and downtrodden. It was not just for the privileged few. It wasn't just for the religious keepers of the law like the Pharisees or Sadducees. The message of God is for all who would hear it. Those who are hopeless need hope and finally, in this reading of scripture, Jesus is saying that the God of hope had arrived. He was now on the scene. The poor would hear the good news and be blessed.

It is interesting to note that God has always had a heart for the outcast. He is "no respecter of persons." Not long after I gave my life to the Lord, I began to feel the call to full-time ministry. The enemy wasted no time in pointing out all of my flaws, past sins, and inadequacies. The fear and self loathing began to creep in as I asked myself "How can God use someone as bad as me for anything?" I had spent a few years drinking, partying and living a life of rebellion.

Then, just when I was about to accept the lie that God would not and could not use me for his glory, God gave me a revelation from His Word. He began to shed light on certain passages of Scripture where God picked deeply flawed and sinful men and women to serve and glorify Him. Men and women like David, Moses, Abraham, Rahab, Samson, and Solomon. David had Uriah killed for a woman he committed adultery with, Moses murdered the Egyptian, Abraham lied about Sarah, Rahab was a prostitute, Samson was given to drinking and womanizing, and Solomon married pagan wives and allowed their gods worshipped in God's holy city! Yet, in spite of their flaws God used them all. He even called David a man after His own heart! God often picks those we wouldn't pick for anything to be His greatest generals. His greatness is shown in our weakness. Our love is great for we have been forgiven much. Oh, how God loves the afflicted, the poor, the outcasts.

God went to me when I was "afflicted" when I was "spiritually sick" and loved me right where I was. The good news comes rushing over the poor and afflicted. Praise God! Sadly, this is because the rich and seemingly unafflicted are to busy with themselves and pondering their own greatness and success to see the King of Glory in front of them. I am thankful that so very often, God brings me to a place where I am broken enough to get a fresh revelation of Him. A place where I can behold Him and thus be transformed by His greatness. I believe that the good news can only be accepted by those who are "empty" or "poor." Only then can He fill us. And only then can we overflow to the world around us as we are called to do.

To Proclaim Release To The Captives

Jesus came to proclaim Release to the Captives. We know from Scripture that when Jesus spoke it was not just His words going forth. Jesus says only what the Father tells Him to say and does only what the Father tells Him to do. Jesus went forth anointed by the Father with full authority and proclaimed release to those held captive by sin and the lies of the enemy.

The enemy has for too long kept as his own what by right belongs to Jesus Christ. Do you know that you are a child of God. You are precious to the Father. God's Word tells us that we are called "sons of God" when we are born again and in Christ. We are clothed in His righteousness and co heirs with Him. Most of us as Christians know this theologically even if we are not walking in the fullness of this truth. Do you know though that God loved you even before you were saved? Even before you were born He loved you. Before the foundation of the world He conceived you in His imagination, in His mind and you were conceived in love. Not just in love, but divine love! Scripture tells us that Jesus was sent to this world that all might be saved and reconciled to the Father. Do you believe that?

The Father has come for His Children! He wants them back in His arms, in His house, and He has sent Jesus to bring them back. For the Bible tells us that Jesus is the *way*, the truth and the life. He is the *way* back to the Father! Jesus came to proclaim release to those held captive by the enemy and by sin. When Jesus came He brought the message that the kingdom of God was at hand! The cross and the blood of the Lamb has set us free. Let us walk in it fully! So, now I say to you, be released that you might be used to release others, that they might know the Father and His amazing love.

The Recovery Of Sight To The Blind

Jesus gives sight to the blind! This section is very closely related to the above section. For often this recovery of sight comes right alongside the captives released. Let me share with you a story from a crusade I preached at in Epe, Nigeria in 2002. Epe is a city located in Lagos State, which is on the southwest coast of the nation. In this part of Nigeria, it is no secret that the people traditionally worshiped traditional, tribal, spirits, gods and goddesses. And for centuries the people of Epe had annually held a huge festival honoring the "queen of the river" or "queen of the sea."

On the third day of our meetings there, I was taking a nap in the hotel room between sessions. Typically, we would have pastor's conferences in the morning, healing and deliverance in the early afternoon and the city-wide crusade in the evening. As I lay in bed, the Lord gave me a vision of the spiritual happenings of this region. Suddenly I saw a huge hideous creature in the sky, I am not sure, but I think it may have been two. I felt these were demon spirits that had a stronghold on the area. They were blowing smoke from their mouths and noses that was keeping the people from seeing the light of the gospel of Jesus Christ. The gospel was there, and was being preached, but the smoke was blinding the people from receiving the truth. That night in the meetings, I shared this vision and we specifically confronted these demonic powers in the name of Jesus, and from then on we noticed an increase in the fruit of our ministry in the city.

The Lord granted me this vision that we might see better how to do His work. The name of Jesus sent the enemy fleeing and the people of Epe could see more clearly the truth of the gospel. The light began to pierce the darkness and many more were touched by the love of God and came to know the Lord.

Often times here in America, the enemy uses other things to bind us. He uses materialism, lust and greed. All of these are bad enough in their own right, but I believe the number one cause of blindness in America is busyness. This is true not only in the world, but in the church as well.

Our children's lives are often so filled with video games and television they would never think of pondering the existence of God. As adults, we retreat into endless activities and extra-long workdays. We find that our lives are complicated by technology instead of freed by it. We are to busy for life, family and sadly for God. Is this right? Many times I have been awakened to find that I had been temporarily blinded by the busyness of my life. Let us do what we need to do to ensure that our own families and churches will not fall prey to this blindness anymore. In Jesus there is recovery of sight. His light takes away all darkness, and as the Word of God tells us, darkness can not dwell with light.

He has come that the blind would see again! Throughout the history of His church He has used men and women to restore sight to His people. Just in the last few hundred years He has used Martin Luther and John Calvin to reform the church, He used the Moravians to fan the flames of missions and prayer, He used Jonathan Edwards and John Wesley to revive His church again. He used Evan Roberts to spark the Welsh Revival in 1904, and William Seymour at Azusa Street. He has used Billy Graham and Oral Roberts in the twentieth century. He used me in a little way that night in Nigeria, and He will just as surely use you right where you are. You see, you are right were you are for a reason. Let Him use you to restore sight to your friends, families, co-workers and the world. Help them to see Jesus!

To Set Free Those Who Are Oppressed

Jesus sets free those who are oppressed! He did it 2000 years ago and He is doing it today. As we begin the 21st century, oppression remains as much a problem as it has ever been and takes many forms. For the sake of the limitations of this book, I will focus on the most common form of oppression that the spirit-filled believer will encounter in life and ministry, that of oppression by evil spirits.

A lot of people in the church in the western world do not like to talk about evil spirits. In our civilized and often educated arrogance, some scholars and believers feel that the belief that evil spirits affect people regularly is something to be believed only by ignorant third world people. I wish that were the case, but it is not.

The Bible tells us that enemy is here to steal, kill and destroy. Do we believe this statement? Satan hates you. He hates your family. He wants to destroy you because of who you remind him of. Remember, you are made in the image of God. Because of who your Father is, your enemy Satan will do anything he can to make your life a hell on earth. He wants to bring pain, sadness, sickness, fear, doubt, guilt, bitterness, anger, hate, jealousy, lust, and disease into your home to keep you from fulfilling God's purposes in your life.

God's Word clearly says that Jesus came that we might have life more abundantly. It says that God desires for us to prosper in all things. If Satan and his many demons can get you to pay attention to some problem or circumstance and take your eyes off God, then they can basically torture you and inflict pain on your Father. Do you know that it pains God to see you suffer when He has provided a way out for you through the cross, blood, and resurrection of Jesus. How it breaks my heart when people I care for are suffering and in torment when they have access to freedom in Christ. He who the Son sets free is free indeed!

We need to begin to walk in this freedom as a church. Because only when the church is free from oppression, can we begin to free this world. The church today often seems like we are a big hospital. But instead of opening our doors to bring healing and the love of Jesus to the outside, we are tied up treating and bandaging up ourselves. So we must ask, How do we walk in freedom from oppression.

The first thing we can do is to be aware that the enemy is looking for a way into our lives, homes and churches. We need to pray daily that God will give us eyes to see our weak points. In our times of intimacy with Him, He will make sure our backs are covered. He will bring to light our weaknesses so that we can bring them to Him to heal and fix. Only a daily, intimate walk with the Lord can assure us of this protection.

The second thing we can do is maintain our focus on God and His Word. We need to know God's promises for our lives! In every situation we have decisions to make. Are we going to believe God or our problems? Are we going to believe our circumstances or God's promises that He has given us in His Word? The Spirits of doubt and fear and a hoard of others are just waiting for an open door. We cannot let them get a foothold in our lives, families or church. Focus on Him.

Thirdly, we can ask God in prayer if there are any spirits that are affecting us or our households at the present time. If there are, be sure that God has given you all authority to bind them and cast them out. Forbid them to operate any longer in your life! I promise you they have to listen. At the name of Jesus they will flee. Share your need with other Christians, especially those with an anointing for deliverance ministry. Allow them to strategically pray for you and your household.

Then, when we are set free from oppression, we can begin to bring healing to others. The world needs a healthy and whole church. We are made in the image of God and are being transformed daily into the likeness of our Lord Jesus. Jesus told us to pray that God's will would be done on earth as it is in heaven. God's will is clearly that He would bring freedom to the oppressed. He tells us to ask and we shall receive! Let us ask today to be able to be totally free from the oppression of the enemy. Let us ask today for a revelation of God's love that will empower us to share this love gift. The gift of freedom from Satan and all his schemes to steal, kill, and destroy all we hold dear. We like our Lord, are to be a generation of freedom givers! A generation that revolts against the oppression being enforced upon our world by an enemy that has already been defeated at the Cross.

Christian Living

Every Christian bookstore has a section they usually call "Christian Living." I always find it interesting that they also separate any books characterized as Pentecostal/Charismatic or concerning the gifts of the Spirit into a separate category most often called something like "Charismatic Interests." If Christian living is supposed to be anything, it is supposed to be charismatic.

Jesus led a life filled and empowered by the Holy Spirit and so should His followers. The "normal" Christian life should be anything but normal to that of the world around us. We are to be different. He has called us to be set apart. When you are filled with, and baptized in the Holy Spirit, you are different.

The life of a Christian should naturally be characterized by miraculous testimony of God's goodness and the supernatural. Walking hand in hand with Jesus in your daily life, the impossible becomes the norm. Bill Johnson, the pastor of Bethel Church in Redding, California puts it this way, "It is abnormal for a Christian not to have an appetite for the impossible. It has been written into our spiritual DNA to hunger for the impossibilities around us to bow at the name of Jesus."[23]

I think back on the last two years of my life and the miracles of God's provision, care, leading, and victory, seem to come one after the other. God is so faithful! Jesus said that the kingdom of God is at hand. That means it is here! We need only to step out into it, and acknowledge its existence. Though your problems and your situations are very real and in your face, so much more real is the living God. The kingdom is all around you and you are filled with His Spirit. When we realize that we really have been sent by the King to bring His authority into each and every situation, we will then begin to enjoy the "normal" Christian life. Christian living is supernatural living!

Only Imagine

I would ask you now to imagine something with me if you would. Imagine that the room you are in right now is suddenly filled with the presence of God Himself. You look to the door and Jesus walks in. He walks up to you and sits beside you and says:

" Dear Child, I love you so. Before the foundation of the world I have loved you. I created you for a unique purpose. Only you can fulfill your specific role. Go into all the world and tell all my children my gospel, tell them about me. Tell them I love them. Tell them I have come for them that they might have life more abundantly. Tell them that I desire that they might prosper in all things, and that all the world will soon know that I am Lord and God. Love one another and know that I have given you all authority and power over the enemy. You will cast out demons and lay hands on the sick and they will recover. You are set free from fear, guilt, shame and self-condemnation and I will use you to set others free as well. Through you, My name will be proclaimed and the Father will be glorified greatly. It is not as you have thought in the past. My work is not for some great man or woman of God. My work is for all my children. You are all called to go. I have given you all you need. Go in the fullness of the strength I have given you. Whatever situation you find yourself in, you will have the gift you need, the weapon you need, to defeat the enemy and do my will. You are my precious child. I desire for you to do all these things, and you must go now for it is the last hour."

    The above is not imaginary but true. God has said these things to us in His written Word. If you are a believer, you are in His presence right now. In fact, He indwells your very body. Always be aware of His presence. Make no mistake, He has given you all you need! Remember, Jesus said "As the Father sent me, I also send you.!"

Part Four

The Fruit of Blessing

J ust like love and power, being able to receive God's blessing in every area of your life, comes from being made ready by Him, during close, intimate encounters with the Father. When you meet with God, no matter how often, things happen! We should walk away from every time of intimacy with Him somehow changed for the better. Encounters with God change men and often the course of history.

One needs only to look at the Bible to see that this is true. I encourage you to do a study on your own sometime of just how every person in the Old Testament who met with God was changed. They walked away a different person, often with a new destiny and purpose. They always left with a fresh fire and passion for living and for the things of God. In the New Testament, one need only to look at Saul of Tarsus to see what an encounter with God can do to alter the course of a human life.

When we meet with Him regularly, He imparts wisdom and direction. He helps us put to death our fleshly nature and desires. Especially our selfish motives. Time in the presence of almighty God always brings our faults to the surface. Like Isaiah, when we meet with God we come face to face with our unworthiness. Now, for me, most of my unworthiness is usually shown to be selfishness of some sort. We are by nature selfish and prideful. Time with God brings us first to our knees and then to our faces before Him as we realize His great unselfishness shown to us. He, after all, gave His own life for you.

When God saves us and begins to speak to us of His plans for our lives, we naturally begin to think of ways to bring it all about ourselves. We also begin to think of ways to carry out these divine plans immediately! Well, God's way is often a little different. His plans must be accomplished, but they will be accomplished in His time and not until we are ready.

Maybe the Lord has shown you a great vision of your calling. You know it will take a lot of resources to accomplish this, so you begin to seek God for the finances to bring this vision about. God has all the resources of the world at His disposal, and if it is God's destiny for your life, why the wait? The reason is, He must prepare you. He must, just like with love and power, give you the capacity to handle the anointing of blessing and prosperity upon your life.

If the Lord would give you all those resources that you are so sure you need today, what would you do with them? Have you spent enough time with Him to be sure of His leading? Can you hear His voice clearly enough to know how to best use the resources at your disposal. Have you proven yourself obedient in the past with what He has blessed you with? Have you prayed for wisdom to wield all the gifts He has given you already?

I think a key element to living a life of blessing is obedience. As Christians, we are called to be a blessing. God pours His blessings out upon His church and we are to see that the world is blessed. We are, if I may use a business term, managers of God's blessing and outpouring. God has deposited within us so much already. When we begin to manage and bless others with what we have, we will then be given much more to bless with.

Let's examine a scripture that deals with this principle, I think, better than any other. Matthew 25:14-29 reads:

"For it (the kingdom of heaven), is just like a man about to

The Tree of Intimacy

---

go on a journey, who called his own slaves and entrusted his possessions to them. To one he gave five talents, to another, two, and to another, one, each according to his own ability; and he went on his journey. Immediately the one who had received the five talents went and traded with them, and gained five more talents. In the same manner the one who had received the two talents gained two more. But He who received the one talent went away, and dug a whole in the ground and hid his master's money. Now after a long time the master of those slaves came and setteled accounts with them. The one who had received the five talents came up and brought five more talents, saying, "Master, you entrusted five talents to me. See, I have gained five more talents." His master said to him, "Well done, good and faithful slave. You were faithful with a few things, I will put you in charge of many things; enter into the joy of your master."

Also the one who had received the two talents came up and said, "Master, you entrusted two talents to me. See, I have gained two more talents." His master said to him, "Well done good and faithful slave. You were faithful with a few things, I will put you in charge of many things; enter into the joy of your master."

And the one also who had received the one talent came up and said, "Master, I knew you to be a hard man, reaping where you did not sow and gathering where you scattered no seed. And I was afraid, and went away and hid your talent in the ground. See, you have what is yours."

But his master answered and said to him, "You wicked and lazy slave, you knew that I reap where I did not sow and gathered where I scattered no seed. Then you ought to have put my money in the bank, and on my arrival I would have received my money back with interest. Therefore take away the talent from him, and give it to the one who has ten talents. For to everyone who has, more shall be given, and he will have an abundance; but from the one who does not have, even what he does have shall be taken away."

Now, in this parable, the Lord shares some great insight with us about how things work in His kingdom. First of all, I need to share that a "talent" was a great sum in these times. The Holman Bible Dictionary states that a talent was approximately 3000 shekels or about 75.6 pounds of money.[24] These men were all entrusted with a large amount. Similarly today, the Lord has blessed us all with something and just like the men in the parable it is "according to our own ability." He gives us what He knows we can handle and sees if we will use the wisdom He has given us to manage it.

The man who was given little, was afraid he might lose what little he had, so he did nothing with it. The men who had more, invested their new blessing wisely and were rewarded for their efforts with more of a blessing. God will only give you what you can handle. Pray that He will give you the wisdom to use what you have been blessed with. Pray that you would be sensitive to the leading of His Holy Spirit who might say give to this person or give to this ministry. A lot hangs in the balance of these decisions. As you grow in your ability to bless others according to His will for your life, you will grow in the amount of blessing you will have access to in your own life.

All the resources in the world and in heaven belong to God. I believe that the day is coming when the Lord will take back what the enemy has stolen from His church and give it back to us. This world and all its riches belong to God, not Satan. When we are ready, when have proven that we have the capacity to handle the riches of heaven, he will lavish them upon us. In fact, He is doing it already on the individual level. As you prove He can trust you with the blessings of His kingdom you will see more of them in your life.

Many in the west are blind to the basic principles of giving and it is hampering God's move in our generation. Even though we know in our minds that everything belongs to God, we hold onto our money and resources as though we can better manage them than God. Here is another area that we must believe Him in our hearts and with our actions. James tells us that faith without works is dead. Our actions in giving need to line up with our beliefs.

We think that the tithe is a great sacrifice. We mistakenly think that the tithe is giving. The tithe is simply returning to God what is already His. He commands us to tithe. Look again at the above parable. The one who simply returned what his master had given him was called "wicked" and all he had was stripped from Him. But the ones who invested their blessing could give back more, and more was given unto them.

The key to living a life of God's blessing is this, when He blesses you with finances, give back to Him first as God's Word tells us. Then "give cheerfully" out of love to others as you are led by the Lord to do so. If He tells you to support another ministry or world missions, do it! If He tells you to help a widow or a family in need, do it! Seek His guidance and let the Spirit of God direct your giving and I promise you that you will never lack.

The Lord has chosen His church to be the instrument to bless this earth. Only a revelation of God's love can cause a person to part with their beloved money. When we are in His presence He will give us a love that is even greater than our western God of materialism. Do we think that if we give the 300 dollars to bless the church in India that God can not bless us with enough to make your mortgage payment. How big is your God? Mine is big enough to do both!

I am not rebuking the church, but I want to say in love that God is calling us to give out of loving, cheerful hearts. The Lord has called us to be a blessing to the nations. The church in America has enough money right now to fulfill the great commission. The problem is it is stuck in the pockets of a people that believe that God is going to use someone else to do it. If you are waiting to become rich before you start giving above your tithe, I will let you know now it is never going to happen. Rather as you bless others, you will see God bless you.

It is the same in all forms of ministry. If you wait until you are perfect before you witness to someone, you will never witness to anyone. If you wait until you are without sin to preach, you will never preach. It is Him in you that does it all! It is Jesus who saves, heals, and gives. Let Him give through you! I believe that the church in the end-times is going to be like a funnel. This funnel will be used by God to bless the nations in every way. He will funnel His love, His power and His prosperity through His church. Let Him begin to use you at a new level today!

These principles work around the world regardless of the situation. I have been to churches in America, the richest country on earth, where the people actually believe that God may want them to live paycheck to paycheck. To the contrary, I have been in a church in Nigeria that seats 50,000 people at one time and is full of people who are prospering in the midst of a city where millions live in poverty. God is using that church and others like it to change that nation and the world. They believed God's Word as it relates to experiencing His total blessing and they acted on it!

When the church in America finally believes the promises of God over our situation and circumstances, we will be used to usher in the mighty end-time harvest at lightning speed. When we realize that we are not limited to the boundaries of our own bank account, but have access to all the resources of heaven, we will see more divine visions and destinies come to pass. So often, God speaks to a person of the calling on their life and they see nothing but where they are now. They see only their present situation. So, not realizing what they have access to, they dismiss or set that vision on the shelf. Sadly, many die without realizing their God given dream or destiny.

The windows of heaven are open. When Jesus ascended, the gates did not shut. The Holy Spirit is moving upon the earth. If you will begin today and seek intimate, daily, encounters with Him, His blessing will be showered upon every area of your life. As you lose yourself in love for Him, He will give you a love for His children, He will awaken you to supernatural power, and He will release you to give in a way that will both fulfill all your dreams and desires and bless the nations and your community like you never imagined! Isn't God good! Praise Him! Because of the Cross and the Resurrection of Jesus Christ it is all possible!

The Blessing Of God's Favor

Another aspect of God's blessing upon our lives is God's favor. When we abide in Him, when we come to truly know Him and be known by Him through extended times of intimacy with Him, we will begin to notice an increase of His favor upon our lives. We will see a supernatural grace and favor on all we do for His glory. When you begin to experience this favor, you will find it easier and easier to remember to praise God! You know what I mean. Sometimes, know matter who we are or how spiritual we think we are, things begin to creep into our lives and we have to remember to thank and praise Him.

Well, when you are walking in divine favor, as a child of the King, His praises will be continually on your lips! Beginning in the Old Testament, we see that God set apart for Himself a people, the nation of Israel. When they walked with Him, and honored His commandments, and showed their love for Him, they were showered with His favor and grace. A grace to prosper and to defeat their enemies. God's people were given victory in every situation they encountered when they drew close to Him. The same is true for His people today.

God gives us favor when we are in His will, and we will only know His will for us when we meet with Him regularly. He will withhold no good thing from His children. I remember once in my own life, I thought that maybe God was calling me to full-time pastoral ministry. After all, I was in seminary, and most people thought, including myself, that if you were in seminary you were either supposed to be a teacher or a pastor upon graduation. Unbeknownst to me, God was calling me for a season as an itinerant minister and evangelist. Every time I tried to pursue a pastoral position, the door would close. A couple of times it seemed that the position and situation was perfect and was surely God's will, but again the door closed.

At the same time I was receiving invitations to minister internationally and itinerantly as an evangelist or guest speaker. Whenever I pursued these opportunities to minister, the doors flew wide open! I mean, some amazing things happened. For example, I was invited to Africa to preach some crusade meetings and everything just flew into place. Pat Robertson, the founder of CBN and President of Regent University, where I was attending seminary, met with my wife and I, and prayed over our ministry and for the trip. The finances we needed were miraculously provided, those in authority over me sent me out with their blessing, and the trip went smoothly form start to finish. While there, I met with, presented Bibles to, and prayed for, two Muslim tribal kings that still have very much authority in the region in political matters. We were actually praying in their royal palaces! In our evangelistic meetings many people were saved, delivered and healed. Please understand that I am not bragging, I am simply testifying of God's miraculous favor! We need to testify and tell the world about the God we serve!

Over the next year I noticed similar favor whenever I traveled to minister. For example, on my second trip to Nigeria I was ministering at a healing crusade at an AIDS clinic in the capital city of Abuja. It turns out that the director of the clinic, was also a politician and a close friend of the President's personal pastor. So, he made a phone call and the next day we were invited to worship at the Presidential Villa with President Obasanjo. That's right, the President of Nigeria! By the way, the president taught Sunday School for over a half hour, and is a born again Christian. Following the service, I met with the President's personal pastor and one of his closest advisors. The next week the Queen of England and several other heads of state were invited to the same place and meeting that I was. Talk about God's favor! Here I was, an unknown evangelist from America that when he returned home would spend the next few months working in a heating and air conditioning sales company. If you would have told me a week before, I would be worshipping God with the President of Nigeria, I would have never believed you. I would have said it was impossible! But now I know more than ever that nothing is impossible for our God!

When we move where God wants us to, we meet with His blessing and favor. So many times I hear people say, "I want to know God's will or purpose for my life." Nothing but time in His presence will reveal the answer to you. But He promises that when we come to Him and ask, that He will withhold nothing from us. When you ask Him, He is faithful to answer. Remember, He wants you to accomplish His plan for your life more than you do! And when He reveals that plan to you and you begin to walk it out, you will assuredly meet with His grace and favor at every step. God wants you to be victorious in this life! Without that time with Him, we spend precious years wandering in the wilderness and storms of life. But with Him, the light shines bright enough that even great works in progress like you and I can find the way! His unmerited favor is for you!

Part Five

Invitation To Revival

A look at our society reveals just how comfortable we have become in our world. Honestly, when was the last time you heard an American say the words "Come quickly Lord Jesus!?" Do we, as the early church did, await for His return and presence among us with great anticipation and longing? When we are ready as a church, He will not delay in his coming back. He is preparing His bride, adorning her, decorating her, and when the day has arrived that she is ready, He will come in an instant. Are we ready? I saw a bumper sticker on a car the other day that read, "Jesus is coming! Look Busy!" I remember thinking, "Busy doing what?" What does He want us to do? 1 John 2:18 says, "Children, it is the last hour...." Surely, the times are urgent. It is the last hour and you can just feel in the Spirit that something huge is about to happen.

I believe that true revival is coming to the church. A revival that will be known both inside the church, and outside by the world. Think about it, how many secular people in the world know about Brownsville or Azusa Street? Not too many. But, God is about to send a mighty, end-times revival that will truly touch all flesh, and there are things that we, the church, will do to usher it in. Yes, God can do it without us, but He has shown us throughout His Word in

The Tree of Intimacy

the Bible that He has chosen to use us. God will reveal Himself through His people, His church.

Throughout this small book, I have tried to share a little of what the Lord has revealed to me through times of prayer and my daily walk with Him. I believe that the following is the central message of all I have shared in the preceding chapters.

In the center of your life there is to be a tree, a strong tree with deep roots. This tree is intimacy. It is your personal, private and intimate relationship with the Father. Over time, as you grow in intimacy with Him, as you are transformed more and more into His image, by being with Him, as you truly know Him more and more, the roots of the tree of intimacy grow stronger and deeper. They grow to a depth you need to be at to withstand the coming storms and battles that lie ahead. You have a purpose and He will ensure your strength to carry it out.

As this growth continues, fruit begins to develop in your life. As you cry out passionately to know Him more, you will, and His love becomes more and more a part of your life. You are filled by Him and his love. It refreshes and renews every dry area of your life. You are filled with His love in such a way that it overflows to all that come in your presence. Intimacy with Him transposes His presence upon yours. You begin to look upon the world with new eyes. Eyes of compassion and the love of Jesus. You now begin to see as He sees.

This revelation of love in your life becomes more total and complete as you walk daily in intimacy with Him. You now minister, and pray, and share the gospel as you always have but something is different. Your intimacy with Him cannot be hidden. All those around you notice a difference. You are saturated with His Spirit. He and His goodness flow out of you. When you pray for people and the nations, you pray prayers of love and not merely prayers consisting of words. As God is love, He fills you daily with His love that you might share it with the world. Things begin to change in the heavens and on earth through the love flowing from you.

God's outpouring is like a waterfall or a shower upon us. It comes upon His church vertically, then it is released and flows from us in a horizontal direction as streams of living water. His love, and power, and blessing was never meant to stay with us. It is only given to us that it might be given away. "Freely you have received, now freely give." Together we can stand in the gap for this world and pray today that God will flood the churches in such a way with His love, power, and blessing that the doors will burst open, the walls will crumble, and God's glory will flow into our families, neighborhoods, cities, and nations.

As I mentioned earlier, it is my prayer that you will accept this book as an invitation to revival in your life. It can start with you and it can happen today. You have been chosen. The windows of heaven are open over you and the Holy Spirit is moving among His people. Begin today, start fresh with a new level of intimacy with the Father and watch as all else in your life falls into place.

We say we want to see His glory, we want to see His power, and we want to see His purposes fulfilled in our generation. The only way this vision will be a reality is if we, His people, humble ourselves and seek Him for who He is. If we cry out to Him because we love Him, because He is our God and we are His people, His Word promises us He will hear us from heaven and will not deny us one good thing. His purposes will be fulfilled. His glory will cover this earth. All will know that He is Lord. Won't you let Him use you to the fullest potential that He created you for? No matter who you are or how close you are to Him today, there is so much more He has for you. There is so much more of Him for your life. There is always a deeper place. Just when you think it can't get any better with God, He allows you to go a little bit deeper with Him. He wants to pull you closer today.

There has never been a time such as this! As you live your life radically devoted to pursuing His presence and cultivating a life of intimacy with Him, the angels of heaven and all the saints of ages past are cheering you on. God is pouring out His Spirit on those who walk with Him moment by moment. The kingdom is here! Will you believe and press in to Him, will you take your walk with Him to another level? If you do, I promise you will have no regrets, only a lifetime of enjoying the amazing love, supernatural power and miraculous blessings of God!

Endnotes

[1] Luke 11:9
[2] 1 Thessalonians 5:17
[3] K.P. Yohannan, *A Revolution in World Missions* (Gospel for Asia/gfa books, 1998) 41.
[4] Richard J. Foster, *Celebration of Discipline* (San Francisco: Harper, 1978) 100-101.
[5] Psalm 46:10
[6] Mike Bickle, *After God's Own Heart* (Charisma House, 2004) 6-7.
[7] Bruce Demarest, *Soul Guide* (Colorado Springs: Navpress 2003) 156.
[8] Matthew 6:33
[9] Brother Lawrence, The Practice of The Presence of God (New Kinsington, PA: Whitaker House, 1982) 8.
[10] 1 John 4;16
[11] John 13:35
[12] Mark 4:35-41
[13] John 10:10
[14] Leonard Ravenhill, *Why Revival Tarries* (Bethany Fellowship, 1959) 16.
[15] Barry Adams, The Father's Love Letter Copyright 1999 Father Heart Communications, www.FathersLoveLetter.com. Used By Permission.
[16] Mahesh Chavda, *The Hidden power of The Believer's Touch* (Shippensburg, PA: Destiny Image, 2001) 63.
[17] Rick Joyner, *Mobilizing The Army of God* (New Kinsington, PA: Whitaker House, 1994) 133.

[18] David Cartledge, *Sermon*, Bethel Temple Assembly of God, Hampton, VA. April 25, 2002.

[19] Ibid.

[20] Claudio Freidzon, *Treasure in Jars of Clay* (Creation House, 1999) 192.

[21] Smith Wigglesworth, *Faith That Prevails* (Springfield Missouri: Gospel Publishing House, 1988) 48.

[22] J. Rodman Williams, *Renewal Theology, Vol. 2, Salvation, the Holy Spirit, and Christian Living* (Grand Rapids: Zondervan, 1990) 170.

[23] Bill Johnson, *When Heaven Invades Earth* (Shippensburg, PA: Treasure house, 2003) 25.

[24] *Holman Bible Dictionary*, Trent C. Butler, Gen. Ed. (Nashville: Holman Bible Publishers, 1991) 1403.